CENGAGE Learning

Novels for Students, Volume 6

Staff

Series Editors: Marie Rose Napierkowski and Deborah A. Stanley.

Contributing Editors: Betsy Currier Beacom, Robert Bennett, Karen R. Bloom, Chloe Bolan, Sara L. Constantakis, Sharon Cumberland, Carl Davis, Jane Elizabeth Dougherty, Scott Gillam, Catherine L. Goldstein, Margaret Haerens, Jhan Hochman, Jeremy Hubbell, Motoko Fujishiro Huthwaite, Arlene M. Johnson, David Kelly, Paul Loeber, Nancy C. McClure, Tabitha McIntosh-Byrd, Patrick J. Moser, Wendy Perkins, Diane Telgen, Beverly West, and Donna Woodford.

Editorial Technical Specialist: Karen Uchic.

Managing Editor: Joyce Nakamura.

Research: Victoria B. Cariappa, *Research Team Manager*. Andy Malonis, *Research Specialist*. Julia

C. Daniel, Tamara C. Nott, Tracie A. Richardson, and Cheryl L. Warnock, *Research Associates*. Jeffrey Daniels, *Research Assistant*.

Permissions: Susan M. Trosky, *Permissions Manager*. Maria L. Franklin, *Permissions Specialist*. Sarah Chesney, *Permissions Associate*.

Production: Mary Beth Trimper, *Production Director*. Evi Seoud, *Assistant Production Manager*. Cindy Range, *Production Assistant*.

Graphic Services: Randy Bassett, *Image Database Supervisor*. Robert Duncan and Michael Logusz, *Imaging Specialists*. Pamela A. Reed, *Photography Coordinator*. Gary Leach, *Macintosh Artist*.

Product Design: Cynthia Baldwin, *Product Design Manager*. Cover Design: Michelle DiMercurio, *Art Director*. Page Design: Pamela A. E. Galbreath, *Senior Art Director*.

Copyright Notice

individual does not imply endorsement of the editors or publisher. Errors brought to the attention of the publisher and verified to the satisfaction of the publisher will be corrected in future editions.

Gale Research
27500 Drake Rd.
Farmington Hills, MI 48331-3535

ISBN 0-7876-2115-3
ISSN 1094-3552

Printed in the United States of America.
10 9 8 7 6 5 4 3 2

The House of the Spirits

Isabel Allende 1982

Introduction

Until the publication of Isabel Allende's *House of the Spirits*, few female writers had emerged from the "Boom" of Latin American literature that began in the 1960s. When the translation of *La casa de los espíritus* appeared in 1985, however, Allende received the kind of international attention that had previously been reserved for writers such as Colombian Nobel Prize-winner Gabriel García Márquez. In fact, *The House of the Spirits* has frequently been compared with García Márquez's masterpiece *One Hundred Years of Solitude* because of Allende's mixture of magical and realistic elements and her multi-generational plot. While there are some similarities between the two works, *The House of the Spirits* is distinguished by its author's unique perspective as a woman and a Chilean.

The novel follows three generations of Trueba women—Clara, Blanca, and Alba—as they struggle to establish their independence from Esteban Trueba, the domineering family patriarch. The political backdrop to this family story is the growing conflict between forces of Left and Right, culminating in a military coup that leads to a stifling dictatorship. While the country is never specifically named as Chile, its political history reflects that of the author's homeland. In 1973, military forces deposed the legally elected administration of President Salvador Allende, Isabel's uncle. "I think I have divided my life [into] before that day and after that day," Allende told *Publishers Weekly* interviewer Amanda Smith. "In that moment, I realized that everything was possible—that violence was a dimension that was always around you." Because of this realization, *The House of the Spirits* has a political element that is more explicit than many other works of magic realism. This makes it "one of the best novels of the postwar period, and a major contribution to our understanding of societies riddled by ceaseless conflict and violent change," Bruce Allen observed in the *Chicago Tribune Book World*. "It is a great achievement, and it cries out to be read."

Author Biography

Allende (pronounced "Ah-*yen*-day") was born August 2, 1942, in Lima, Peru, the daughter of Chilean diplomat Tomás Allende and his wife, Francisca Llona Barros. Her father was a first cousin of Salvador Allende, her godfather, who later became president of Chile. Allende's parents divorced when she was just two years old, and her mother took her to live with her grandparents. Allende's grandparents had a profound influence on her, and she has said they served as the models for the characters of Esteban and Clara Trueba in *The House of the Spirits*. Allende's mother later remarried, and her new husband was also a diplomat whose assignments took the family abroad. By the time she was fifteen, the author had lived in Bolivia, Europe, and the Middle East.

Allende became a noted journalist in Chile, authoring regular magazine columns, editing a children's magazine, and even hosting a weekly television program. At the same time, she tried her hand at producing plays and writing short stories for children. Allende married engineer Miguel Frías in 1962, and the couple had two children, Paula and Nicolás. In the meantime, her uncle Salvador Allende was elected President of Chile on his fourth attempt at the office. When his government fell to a military coup on September 13, 1973, the author's life took a dramatic change. Like her character Alba, Allende joined the efforts of church-sponsored groups in providing food and aid to the needy and families of the victims of the regime. For fifteen months, the author helped many people escape the military's persecution at the risk of her own life, witnessing events that she would later incorporate into her first novel. "Because of my work as a journalist I knew exactly what was happening in my country, I lived through it, and the dead, the tortured, the widows and orphans, left an unforgettable impression on my memory," the author wrote in *Discurso Literario*. "The last chapters of *La casa de los espíritus* narrate those events. They are based on what I saw and on the direct testimonies of those who lived through the brutal experience of the repression."

Because of her family connections, Allende lost her job, and fear for their safety led her family to flee Chile for Caracas, Venezuela in 1975. Despite her considerable experience as a journalist, she found it difficult to find work as a writer. Instead she worked as a teacher and administrator for several years before taking a position with one of the leading newspapers in the country. The exiled author felt isolated, however, and was concerned about the ailing grandfather she had left behind. Wanting him to know she had not forgotten him, she began writing a letter recounting all the family stories she had learned. This letter turned into the manuscript for her first novel, *La casa de los espíritus*, and after finding a Spanish agent, the work was published in 1982. Despite being banned in Chile, copies found their way to Chilean readers, and the novel earned worldwide popularity upon translation.

Allende's subsequent works have gained similar success with critics and readers. *De amor y sombra* (1984; translated as *Of Love and Shadows),* *Eva Luna* (1987), and *Cuentos de Eva Luna* (1990; translated as *Stories of Eva Luna*) all take place in Latin America or the Caribbean and deal with similar themes of love, literature, and survival. Her 1991 work *El plan infinito* (translated as *The Infinite Plan*) takes place in America. The author herself relocated to the United States in 1988, having married American lawyer William Gordon that year. Allende also used her own experiences as inspiration for writing the 1995 autobiography *Paula*, which recounts the author's thoughts as she sat by her dying daughter's bedside. Despite her continuing success, she remains best known for her first work, *The House of the Spirits*.

Clara

The House of the Spirits begins by introducing readers to Severo and Nívea del Valle and two of their daughters: Rosa, the oldest, and Clara, the youngest. Clara, who has been denounced by the local priest as possessed by the devil, predicts a death in the del Valle family, which is tragically fulfilled when Rosa accidentally drinks poison meant for Severo. As a result of Rosa's death, her fiancé Esteban Trueba, who has been working at the mines hoping to make his fortune, tells his sister Férula that he will instead restore their family's estate, Tres Marías. During his tenure there, Esteban rapes one of the tenants on his estate, Pancha García, and impregnates her, a pattern he will continue with other women on the estate. After he has had relations with all the young women on the estate, Esteban begins going to the local brothel, where he meets Tránsito Soto and assists her by giving her fifty pesos to leave town.

After nine years in the countryside, Esteban returns to the city to see his dying mother and is betrothed to Clara, who has recently broken a nine-year silence by announcing that she will marry Rosa's fiancé. Clara gives birth to a daughter, Blanca, and twin boys whom she names Jaime and Nicolás against Esteban's wishes. Esteban meets

Tránsito Soto again and she tells him she wants to start a whores' cooperative. After finding his sister Férula in bed with Clara, Esteban banishes her from the house, and Clara's clairvoyant powers fail in locating her. When the family is at Tres Marías, Férula appears as a ghost and Clara insists on returning to the city, knowing that Férula is dead.

Blanca

When next the Truebas return to Tres Marís, Blanca and her childhood playmate Pedro Tercero García begin a love affair. Clara divines that Blanca is having an affair after a massive earthquake which breaks all of Esteban's bones. Following the earthquake, Pedro García sets Esteban's bones, his son Pedro Segundo becomes foreman of the estate, and his grandson Pedro Tercero begins preaching socialist ideas to the tenants. Clara takes on the domestic duties of the estate, working closely with Pedro Segundo and shutting the city house. Esteban fires Pedro Tercero for insubordination, but he and Blanca continue their affair. When Count Jean de Satigny, a guest at the estate, asks for Blanca's hand, she refuses him. Soon after the death of Pedro García, Jean tells Esteban that Pedro Tercero and Blanca are lovers. After Clara points out that though they are like Esteban in taking lovers from other social classes, Blanca and Pedro Tercero have done so out of love, an enraged Esteban hits her. Pedro Segundo leaves Esteban's employ and Esteban swears revenge on Pedro Tercero, finding him with the help of Esteban García, his own illegitimate grandson. After he chops off three of Pedro Tercero's fingers, Esteban refuses Esteban García the reward he has promised him.

Esteban orders Jean de Satigny to marry the pregnant Blanca. Clara assures Blanca that Pedro Tercero still lives, and also predicts that Esteban Trueba will win his election by a small margin. Meanwhile, Blanca's brother Jaime, a doctor who helps the poor and disagrees with his father's conservative politics, performs an abortion on Nicolás' girlfriend Amanda, whom he secretly loves. By the time she gives birth to her daughter Alba, Blanca has discovered her husband's erotic photographs of the servants and has left him. Alba grows up thinking that her father has died, but Blanca continues her affair with her true father, Pedro Tercero. As a child, Alba has her first encounter with Esteban García, who nearly molests her.

Alba

Clara dies on Alba's seventh birthday and her grieving husband begins to shrink. After his son Nicolás' naked protest gives Esteban a heart attack, he gives Nicolás money to leave the country. Esteban constructs a mausoleum for Clara and Rosa and when he kisses Rosa's corpse, it disintegrates in his hands. Esteban becomes obsessed with the "Marxist cancer," but Blanca continues to see Pedro Tercero, now a popular singer of socialist songs, though she will not marry him because she is afraid of losing her class status. Esteban meets Tránsito Soto again and murmurs Clara's name while he has sex with her.

At the university, Alba joins Miguel's political cause out of love for him, and when she is unmasked as Esteban Trueba's granddaughter by Esteban García, Miguel's love for her overcomes his sense of betrayal. Jaime leaves his father's house because he supports the Candidate and agrees to help Miguel's drug-addicted sister, his lost love Amanda. The Candidate becomes the President, and Pedro Tercero joins the government, after which Blanca rejects his final marriage proposal. Esteban Trueba is helping to sabotage the economy, but the younger Truebas work for the survival of the new government. After the peasants of Tres Marías take Esteban prisoner, Blanca and Alba ask Pedro Tercero to rescue him and he agrees. During this visit, Pedro Tercero's love for Blanca is rekindled, while Alba learns that Pedro Tercero is her father. After Pedro Tercero rescues Esteban, they discover their personal hatred is extinguished, but hatred in the rest of the country is on the rise. Jaime is shot and killed during a coup which Esteban celebrates; when Esteban offers his services to the new regime he learns of his son's death and the destruction of the democratic system. Esteban is disgusted with himself after he orders the peasant village at Tres Marías destroyed. After the funeral of the Poet, which becomes the symbolic burial of freedom, Esteban admits that he has made a mistake, enabling Blanca and Pedro Tercero to flee the country and asking her forgiveness, which she grants by telling him she loves him.

Alba's terrible nightmare comes true when she is arrested and tortured by Esteban García, but she refuses to give up Miguel. When Alba is at her lowest point, in solitary confinement, Clara appears to her and tells her to write in order to survive. Meanwhile, on the outside, Esteban gets Transíto Soto to help him secure Alba's release. After the two restore the house and write their story, Esteban dies in Alba's arms. Alba is pregnant, possibly as a result of having been raped, and she realizes that her grandfather's evil created the evil of Esteban García and vows to break that terrible chain. Alba is left, at the end of the novel, waiting for Miguel's return and her daughter's birth.

Characters

Amanda

With her "exotic appearance"—long black hair, heavily made-up eyes, and beaded necklaces—Amanda is passionately loved by both Trueba brothers. Amanda has a "free, affectionate, adventurous" personality, yet is practical enough to realize the immature and selfish Nicolás is not a good match for her. She has a "very old soul," aged prematurely by her extreme poverty and her responsibility for her young brother Miguel. While it is Jaime who would be able to take care of her, it is twenty years before the two begin a relationship. By this time, unfortunately, Jaime no longer feels capable of any deep emotion but compassion. Amanda joins him at the clinic, and works there even after his death. During the terror she is detained by the police and questioned about her brother's revolutionary activities. Weakened by her grief and her years of drug use, she dies in custody without betraying her brother, just as she had promised him years before.

Barrabás

Barrabás arrives at the del Valle household with the rest of Uncle Marcos's effects, barely recognizable as a puppy. Clara recognizes him at once for what he is, adopts him, and nurses him back to health. The huge dog seems to be the living embodiment of the mythical beasts Rosa embroiders on her tablecloth. He is devoted to Clara, even accompanying her on sleepwalks, and dies on her engagement day, stabbed in the back with a butcher's knife.

Countess

See Alba Trueba

Nívea del Valle

Clara's mother, Nívea, is a good example of the first stage of feminism in Chile. She demonstrates for women's rights while still being a dutiful mother of fifteen. While she jokes with her friends that women will not have the strength to take advantage of their rights as long as they wear corsets and long skirts, "she herself was not brave enough to be among the first to give up the fashion." She treats her favorite daughter, Clara, "as if she were an only child, creating a tie so strong that it continued into succeeding generations as a family tradition." Nívea dies in a car accident with her husband, Severo, in which she is decapitated. Clara locates the head after others are unable to find it, and after spending years in the Trueba basement it is eventually buried with Clara in the mausoleum.

Rosa del Valle

The oldest of the del Valle daughters, Rosa is

"the most beautiful creature to be born on earth since the days of original sin." She has yellow eyes and green hair, and has a "maritime grace" that makes her resemble a mermaid. She becomes Esteban Trueba's fiancée because he is the only man brave enough to approach her. Nevertheless, while he is away making his fortune, Rosa scarcely thinks of him as she dreamily embroiders strange creatures on an endless tablecloth. Her mother senses that Rosa "was not destined to last very long in the vulgar traffic of this world" and so she learns nothing about managing a household. Nívea's premonition is accurate, for Rosa is killed with a flask of poisoned brandy meant for her father. She is even more beautiful in death, and decades later is completely unchanged when Esteban Trueba steals her body to place it in the family mausoleum.

Severo del Valle

Clara's father, Severo, is "an atheist and a Mason," but since he has political ambitions he attends church faithfully. He joins the Liberal party despite being a member of the upper class, and is invited to run as a Congressional representative for a southern district "that he had never set foot in and had difficulty finding on a map." He gives up his lifelong political ambitions, however, after his daughter Rosa is poisoned. He ironically wishes that "none of his descendants would ever get mixed up in politics," although that is exactly what happens. Severo dies in a car accident, a victim of his "weakness for modern inventions."

Alba de Satigny

See Alba Trueba

Count Jean de Satigny

The Count de Satigny is a frequent visitor to Esteban Trueba's home at Tres Marías. While some people mock his concern with appearance and etiquette, he still becomes a figure of high social standing. After Blanca refuses his marriage proposal, he is considerate enough to win her friendship. When he discovers the true nature of Blanca's relationship with Pedro Tercero, however, he betrays them to Esteban, leading to a terrible family fight. A few months later, when Esteban learns Blanca is pregnant, he forces the Count to marry her and legitimize the child. "He did not know whether to feel sorry for himself for having fallen victim to these savage aborigines, or to rejoice at being on the verge of fulfilling his dream of marrying a rich, young, beautiful South American heiress." Satigny settles for the second interpretation, but the marriage does not last long. When Blanca discovers the Count's collection of pornographic photographs, she leaves without looking back. The family never hears from him again until called to identify his body, felled by a stroke during old age.

Ana Díaz

Ana is one of Alba's fellow students at the

university, and is somewhat disdainful when she learns that Alba is the granddaughter of Esteban Trueba. She is more understanding when they meet again as captives of the police. She is "indomitable," and helps Alba survive her captivity. It is Ana who gives Alba a notebook and suggests she write everything down to "get out whatever's worrying you inside, so you'll get better once and for all."

Esteban García

Because of his grandmother Pancha's reminders, Esteban García grows up keenly aware that he is the grandson of Esteban Trueba, even if his grandfather scarcely notices his existence. He first comes to Trueba's notice when he offers to reveal the hiding place of Pedro Tercero. Trueba gives him a slap instead of a reward, however, leaving the boy weeping with rage. When young Esteban comes to ask his grandfather for help in entering the police force, he molests Alba, recognizing "she embodied everything he would never have, never be." On her fourteenth birthday he gives Alba her first "kiss," giving her nightmares of a green beast trying to suffocate her. His hatred is cemented when she orders him to take her home after leaving the university strike. After the coup he becomes a colonel and Alba becomes his private prisoner, there for him to "avenge himself for injuries that had been inflicted on him from birth."

Pancha García

The daughter of Pedro García, Pancha is just fifteen when Esteban first spots her working on the plantation. A peasant of Indian extraction, she "had the beauty of early youth," although Esteban could see "that it would quickly fade, as it does with women who are born to have many children, work without rest, and bury their dead." Esteban uses and then discards Pancha, even as she bears him a child. Her son Esteban is the only bastard he admits is his, even though he sires many more with the women of Tres Marías. Pancha later dies of chicken fever, beyond the help of her father Pedro's remedies.

Pedro García

Pedro is an elderly man when Esteban Trueba takes over the operation of Tres Marías. He claims his grandfather had fought for independence against the Spaniards and tells marvelous stories. He knows almost as much about herbs and healing as the *curandera*, and it is Pedro García and not the gringo technician who finds the cure for the ant plague. It is also old blind Pedro who sets Esteban's bones "so perfectly that the doctors who examined Trueba afterward could not believe such a thing was possible." He dies an old man, of sound mind and clear memory although blind and deaf.

Pedro Segundo García

The son of Pedro García, Pedro Segundo ("the

Second") becomes the foreman on the Tres Marías plantation, a position which "brought him no more privileges, but only more work." Although he is most likely the same age as Esteban Trueba, he "looked older." Pedro Segundo is more intelligent than the other peasants, but Trueba never treats him as a friend and Pedro Segundo looks on his *patrón* with a "mixture of fear and resentful admiration." He is loyal and dependable, however, and never speaks against Trueba or his policies. Clara learns to treat him as a friend and partner when she takes charge of the plantation after the earthquake, and Pedro Segundo "valued her as much as he detested Esteban Trueba." He comforts her after Trueba knocks her teeth out over her defense of Blanca's relationship with Pedro Tercero. Pedro Segundo never sees any of the family after that point, for he leaves the plantation rather than witness what might happen when Trueba takes his revenge on his son.

Media Adaptations

- Danish director Bille August made a film version of *The House of the Spirits* starring Jeremy Irons as Esteban, Meryl Streep as Clara, Glenn Close as Férula, Antonio Banderas as Pedro Tercero, and Winona Ryder as Blanca. The film was not particularly successful, with many critics claiming the Anglo actors were hopelessly miscast. One critic even suggested that the only worth of the adaptation was as a "potential camp cult film."

Pedro Tercero García

Although he physically resembles his father, Pedro Segundo, Pedro Tercero ("the Third") is willing to defy Esteban Trueba and fight against the injustice of the social order. Despite his father's beatings and Trueba's warnings, Pedro Tercero continues to discuss "revolutionary" ideas of justice he learns from Leftist leaning teachers, priests, and union members. But while he believes he must struggle against injustice, he also "knew his place in the world"—one that will never allow him to have a legitimate relationship with the daughter of Esteban Trueba. When Trueba discovers his secret affair with Blanca, Pedro is forced to hide from the *patrón*'s anger. A confrontation leads to Pedro Tercero losing three fingers to Trueba's ax. He recovers and learns to play the guitar again and soon is recording songs of revolution that make him famous. Although his fame brings him many women, none of them is Blanca's equal. He begins to secretly meet with her once again, but she refuses to allow him to recognize Alba as his daughter and turns down his proposals. Even though he is "disillusioned with political organizations" and "had no ambition for either money or power," after the Candidate's election he is drawn into an administrative post in the government. The pressures of the job lead him to give Blanca a final ultimatum: marry him or never see him again. When she refuses again they remain apart for two years, until she asks his help in rescuing her father from the revolutionary tenants who have taken him hostage. Esteban Trueba returns the favor after the coup makes Pedro Tercero a fugitive, arranging for him to escape the country with Blanca. The two live in exile in Canada, where finally "they both felt completely fulfilled in the peace of satisfied love."

Sebastián Gómez

Sebastián Gómez is a professor at the university which Alba attends. He assists the students with their occupation of a university building during the strike, and is naively hopeful that students and workers all over the country will join their cause. He never complains during the occupation, although he wears braces on his crippled legs. Although he is an "ideologue" against injustice, he still believes that women should not be involved in "men's affairs" such as the strike. His naive idealism also leads him to declare that the government is "not a dictatorship and it never will be." Ironically, he is betrayed by his students and is killed by the political police during the first raid on the university after the coup.

Uncle Marcos

Nívea del Valle's brother, Uncle Marcos is a "weather-beaten and thin" world traveller with a pirate's mustache and the manners "of a cannibal," according to Severo del Valle. His first funeral occurs after he disappears while trying to fly a mechanical bird to the mountains. He returns unharmed, however, and after yet another journey sets up a fortune-telling shop with Clara. Clara is closest to her uncle, not only because of her clairvoyance but because she loves his stories of exotic lands. Uncle Marcos has written accounts of his travels and stores these journals and his books of fairy tales in the family junk room. Although Uncle Marcos dies while Clara is still a child, his stories live on as they entertain and instruct Blanca, Pedro Tercero, and Alba.

Father José Dulce María

Father José Dulce María is a Spanish priest with revolutionary ideas that have led to his being sent to San Lucas, "that hidden corner of the world." He turns Biblical stories into Socialist parables, and is an important influence on Pedro Tercero. He not only teaches the boy philosophy, but also instructs him in "how to cultivate his natural poetic gifts and to translate his ideas into songs." Father José also takes Pedro Tercero in after his encounter with Esteban Trueba and heals him "in both body and soul."

Miguel

Amanda's younger brother Miguel is around five when he first encounters the big Trueba house on the corner. He calls Clara "Mama" and Jaime "Papa" and is inseparable from his sister until Clara convinces her to allow him to attend school. As an adult, he is a revolutionary who believes violence is the only way to effect radical change. He is a natural leader, and during the building occupation "seemed to be the only one who knew what to do." He loves Alba even after he discovers she is the "bourgeois" granddaughter of Esteban Trueba, and they create a love nest in the basement of the big house. Nevertheless, Miguel realizes that Alba's commitment to the cause is for love, not political conviction, and insists that she remain uninvolved in any of his guerilla activities. Jaime believes that Miguel is one of those with a "dangerous idealism and an intransigent purity that color everything they touch with disaster," but he is fond of the young man because of his "natural gaiety" and "capacity for tenderness." After the coup, Miguel goes into hiding and manages to evade capture. He is also the one who comes up with the idea to use Tránsito Soto to arrange Alba's release. It is implied in the

Epilogue that Miguel will remain in Chile as long as he has to in order to bring about the political change he so passionately wants.

Mora Sisters

The three Mora sisters "were the only people who possessed irrefutable proof that souls can take on physical form." They learn of Clara's existence through "telepathic contact" with her, and are soon frequent visitors at the big house. Nicolás spends quite a bit of time with them during his unsuccessful attempts to develop his own powers of perception, and it is through them that he meets Amanda. The sisters are associated with the scent of wild violets, which is how their presence is announced at several points in the novel. It is the last surviving sister, Luisa Mora, who prophetically warns Alba of the danger that waits for her if she remains in the country after the coup.

Nana

Nana is the Indian caretaker of all the children in first the del Valle and later the Trueba family. After Rosa's death, it is Nana who is able to comfort the guilty Severo del Valle, who believes the poison was intended for him: "He felt that this woman, as warm and generous as the earth itself, would be able to console him." She is an important member of the del Valle and Trueba households, and yet apart, born to "live on borrowed happiness and grief" without ever truly having her own life. She dies of fright during the earthquake, and the chaos caused by the disaster ensures that "none of the many children she had raised with so much love attended her funeral."

Tránsito Soto

Esteban Trueba first meets Tránsito when she is a "skinny adolescent" working at the Red Lantern brothel in the countryside. She has the voice of a "hoarse bird" and a tattoo of a snake around her navel. Esteban likes her because of her practical nature and her "amusing" claim that she will go far in life. When he lends her fifty pesos, he does not know that her repayment of the debt will come to be an important one. She uses the money to move to the city, lead a successful prostitutes' cooperative, and obtain wealth and power. It is ironic that Trueba admires her so, for her success comes from feminine empowerment and Socialist practices.

Alba Trueba

Alba is the product of Blanca's illicit affair with Pedro Tercero García, although she does not learn her true parentage until she is an adult. Her name, which can be translated as "dawn," forms the "last in a chain of luminous words" that serve as names for the women in the novel. She has greenish hair, like her great-aunt Rosa, but otherwise she looks like no other member of the family. Like her predecessors, Alba is also a solitary child, preferring to play imaginary games in the basement of the big house or with her uncle Jaime. Like her grandmother, she has a "wild imagination" and enjoys Uncle Marcos's tales, told as variations by her mother Blanca. She becomes the only focus for Esteban's love and tenderness, since he has already destroyed his relationships with the rest of the family. He agrees that she should have a decent education, since she is "too plain to attract a well-to-do husband."

Alba attends university and despite her grandfather's warnings to avoid love, falls instantly for Miguel, a brash young law school student. She follows him to student protests but manages to keep her activities—including a love nest in the basement —secret from her grandfather. Alba has the same generous spirit as her grandmother, for she smuggles Blanca's hoarded food supplies out to the poor and also gives many of the weapons hidden by her grandfather to Miguel's guerilla movement. After the coup, she helps victims of political persecution find asylum and works with local priests to help feed the poor. "She realized that they had returned to the old days when her Grandmother Clara went to the Misericordia District to replace justice with charity." Her efforts convince Esteban that something has gone wrong in the country, especially after the secret police seize her in the middle of the night. She is tortured, but a vision of Clara convinces her that survival should be her goal. With the aid of Ana Díaz and other women in the prison, Alba recovers and begins to write. Upon her return home, she recreates the family story at her grandfather's urging, so "you'll be able to take your roots with you if you ever have to leave." The act of writing, she discovers, will help her "reclaim the past and overcome terrors of my own," and so she begins with the first lines of her grandmother's diary: *Barrabás came to us by sea …*

Blanca Trueba

The oldest child and only daughter of Esteban and Clara, Blanca looks like an armadillo when she is born. She soon flourishes under Clara's care, and is very close to her mother, as the similarity of her name (which translates as "white") suggests. Her mother treats her as an adult, and as a result, as a very young child "Blanca looked like an intelligent midget" because of her ability to speak and take care of herself. She is still a child when she first meets Pedro Tercero at Tres Marías, and she runs naked to play with the boy and falls asleep on his stomach. This incident foreshadows their future relationship, when they become lovers and are discovered in the same position by Esteban. As a child, Blanca is romantic and sentimental and considered "timid and morose" by her teachers. Only in the country, when she is with Pedro Tercero, does she bloom and become happy. She exchanges secret messages with him and sneaks out of her room to meet him by the river. The commotion when her father discovers their relationship causes the family to split apart.

Blanca is pregnant, however, and when her father discovers this he tells her he has killed Pedro

Tercero and forces her to marry Count Jean de Satigny. She is "a practical, worldly, diffident woman" with a "modern, pragmatic character," so she tries to make the most of her marriage and lead the "idle life that was her true vocation" until discovering the Count's unpleasant hobby. She only loves Pedro Tercero, but refuses to run away with him, not wishing to give up her social position or face the ridicule of his working-class friends. For romantic Blanca, her "poetic fantasies" are better than discovering that "the grandiose love that had withstood so many tests would not be able to withstand the most dreadful test of all: living together." Her refusals separate them for a time, but they reunite over the crisis of her father's kidnapping. The repression after the coup finally forces Blanca to make a decision: she hides Pedro Tercero from the police and then enlists her father's help in escaping the country. Only then can the two men overcome the hatred that had poisoned their lives until then, and Blanca ends up a successful artist in Canada, living "completely fulfilled in the peace of satisfied love."

Clara del Valle Trueba

The youngest of the del Valle children, Clara has an unusual ability to see things, just as her name (which translates as "white" or "clear") suggests. As a child she is "extremely precocious and had inherited the runaway imagination of all the women in her family," and enjoys the stories and books of her Uncle Marcos. Her family accepts her ability to move saltcellars and predict earthquakes, only becoming concerned when the local priest claims she is possessed by the devil. When she witnesses the autopsy of her sister Rosa, it fills her with "the silence of the entire world" and she stubbornly remains mute for the next nine years. Instead she reads voraciously and writes in her notebooks, diaries which prove to be invaluable to her granddaughter Alba in the future. To the dismay of her politically ambitious father, Clara's psychic abilities increase as she grows older, but her mother realizes that the only way to deal with her unusual daughter is to "love her unconditionally and accept her as she was." She is allowed to keep to herself and "in later years would recall her childhood as a luminous part of her existence."

At age nineteen, however, Clara sees her future is with Esteban Trueba and decides she will "marry without love." Esteban, in contrast, falls deeply in love with the woman who has the advantage of charm, if not beauty, over her late sister Rosa. Clara is not a very good manager, being too distracted by the "world of apparitions," and leaves the running of the household to her sister-in-law Férula. After Blanca's birth and the family's move to Tres Marías, however, "she seemed to have been cured of her habit of speaking with invisible spirits and moving the furniture by supernatural means." She works to educate the people on the plantation, trying to teach the women about equality. After Férula's departure and the earthquake, she becomes a more practical person, as the death and destruction she witnesses "put her in touch with the basic needs to which she had been oblivious." She often invokes Esteban's anger and frustration, but is able to defuse his temper with either a few short words or her own inattentiveness. When she supports Blanca's relationship with Pedro Tercero, however, Esteban loses control and strikes her, knocking out several teeth. She refuses to speak to her husband ever again, and moves back to the big house in the city. She resumes her psychic experiments, but is sadder than before. She dies on Alba's seventh birthday, having made up her mind to die. She believes that "dying is like being born: just a change," and Esteban believes that she walks the halls of the big house after her death. This may just be a manifestation of his guilt and desire, however, for it is only after Clara's death that he allows himself to tell her "everything I couldn't say before."

Esteban Trueba

The patriarch of the Trueba family, Esteban is a passionate, hard-working man who is determined to succeed. He is also quick to anger, frequently cruel, and intolerant of those less fortunate than himself. He allows no contradiction of his strict conservative beliefs, and thinks he is justified in ruling his plantation with an iron hand because he has improved the peasants' standard of living. "It would be lovely if we were all created equal, but the fact is we're not," he says, arguing that his workers would be lost without him. He takes the same attitude toward women, wanting to possess Clara "absolutely, down to her last thought," taking advantage of plantation women, and declaring that a woman's duty is "motherhood and the home." His greatest failing is his inability to control his temper, which leads him to hurt those he loves the most. To his regret he always "gets carried away with his punishment," as when he whips Blanca after discovering her with Pedro Tercero or when he beats Clara when she defends her daughter. When Tres Marías is returned to him after the coup, he dismisses all the tenants and burns down the buildings he once worked so hard to build. Afterwards, "despite the pleasure of his revenge, he was unable to sleep. He felt like a father who has punished his children too severely."

Having come from a noted but impoverished household, Esteban is ambitious for both power and money. He is successful in achieving both, becoming a wealthy *patrón* and senator. He is less successful in his personal life, however. His relationships with his children "only worsened with time," and after Clara's death, he notes that he had "only two friends" to try to cheer him up. Férula's curse seems to come true and he shrinks with time. It would be hard to feel sympathy for Esteban, except for two things: the first-person narration that shows how deeply he both loves and suffers; and the tolerance and understanding he finds in his old age. The consequences of the coup have taught him that his judgment is not perfect, and he is not so adamant in having his way. His granddaughter Alba has also mellowed his demeanor, for he has "transferred all his finest sentiments to Alba" and treats her with tolerance and indulgence. He makes no protests over her relationship with Miguel, an orphaned revolutionary, and also mends his differences with Pedro Tercero and Blanca. Thus a man who lived with so much passion and violence dies a peaceful death, "without pain or anguish, more lucid than ever and happy, conscious, and serene."

Ester Trueba

Esteban and Férula's mother has been so afflicted with arthritis that she is "like a living corpse." She came from a rich family, but fell in love with and married a "good-for-nothing" immigrant instead of a man of her own class. Her family's money squandered, Ester Trueba is left to the care of her son Esteban and daughter Férula. She dies bedridden and suffering from gruesome wounds, leaving her son guilty and angry "at not having loved her and cared for her enough."

Férula Trueba

Esteban's sister Férula has spent her life taking care of her mother, and it has left her bitter and resentful. Esteban observes that she was a "beautiful woman," but "already the ugliness of resignation could be glimpsed through her pale, peach-toned skin." While she "took pleasure in humiliation" and performs her duties without complaint, she knows just how to make the recipients of her service feel guilty. She is prepared to hate her new sister-in-law, but Clara's openness disarms her and Férula becomes her most devoted friend. As passionate as her brother, Férula "was one of those people who are born for the greatness of a single love," and it is only with Clara that she permits herself "the luxury of giving in to her overwhelming desire to serve and be loved." Her passion leads her to be jealous of her brother, and the conflict between them causes Esteban to send her away. Six years later her ghost leads the family to her impoverished apartment, where she has obviously refused to use any of the funds sent by her brother. Even in death, she fills Esteban with anger over "her spirit of sacrifice, her severity, her vocation for poverty, and her unshakable chastity, which he felt as a reproach."

Jaime Trueba

One of the twin sons of Esteban and Clara, Jaime has the same desire to help the unfortunate as his mother had. He displays an early interest in the writings of Karl Marx, and as an adult is "tall, robust, timid, and studious." Although he is "peevish" and dislikes dealing with people, he is "generous and candid and had a tremendous capacity for kindness." He creates a tunnel of books in his room in the big house, and studies medicine so that he may help the poor. He ignores his father's disapproval and attends Socialist meetings and, unknown to his father, is the best friend of Pedro Tercero. His one passion is for his brother's lover Amanda, whose "vulnerability was more seductive than anything that had attracted him before." His love for Nicolás is greater than that for Amanda, however, and by the time they begin a relationship, twenty years after first meeting, he is no longer capable of feeling anything but compassion for her. His work with the poor brings him into contact with the President, and so he is with the leader on the day of the coup. He refuses to lie about the President's death, and so the military tortures and executes him. Jaime, who was "preoccupied and more or less continued to be until the day they killed him," provides another example of a person who believes "it can never happen here."

Nicolás Trueba

One of the twin sons of Esteban and Clara, Nicolás "inherited the adventurous spirit of his great-uncle Marcos and his mother's propensity for making up astrological charts and reading the future." He is "as pretty as a girl" and is much smarter than his brother, but Jaime frequently serves as his protector. As a young man Nicolás is interested in girls and the supernatural, trying to develop his powers by studying with the Mora sisters despite his father's insistence that such matters are for women. He has no talent, however, and turns to business ventures such as a dancing school, selling advertising on a zeppelin, and selling chicken sandwiches. He is an innocent, however, as Amanda tells him when he offers to marry her and legitimize their child: "Can't you see my soul is very old and you're still a child?" He searches for spiritual fulfillment in yoga, drugs, travel, and vegetarianism, and in writing a book on the names of God and the attainment of nirvana. He teaches Alba to conquer fear through visualizing it, and sets up an academy called the "Institute for Union with Nothingness." The embarrassment he causes his father leads Esteban to banish him from the country with enough money to settle down. Nicolás founds another institute in North America, and there finds success in combining his quest for God with his skill in business.

Love and Passion

While most of the characters of *The House of the Spirits* experience passionate love, they often discover that passion is not enough to sustain a relationship. Esteban has a deep passion for his wife Clara, but his love is possessive: "he wanted far more than her body; he wanted control over that undefined and luminous material that lay within her." His desire to control what he loves fuels his anger, leading him to punish those he loves when they do not comply with his expectations. Férula's love for Clara similarly becomes a "jealous passion that resembled that of a demanding husband more than it did that of a sister-in-law," and leads to her banishment from the house. But unpossessive love is not complete, either, unless it is tempered with common sense. Amanda, for instance, knows that Nicolás is too immature to make a good husband and refuses to turn their "free love" relationship into a marriage. Blanca is unable to run away with Pedro Tercero because she fears her "grandiose love" will not survive the commonplace nature of everyday life together. Instead, she "fed [her love] with fantasies, idealized it, savagely defended it, stripped it of prosaic truth, and turned it into the kind of love one found in novels." The most successful loves portrayed in the novel are unconditional, involving both giving and receiving. Alba and Miguel love each other without restrictions or conditions, which allows their love to survive his periods of concealment as well as her torture and imprisonment. This healthy attitude toward love is also expressed in parent-child relationships. Nívea del Valle, for instance, understands that the best way to deal with Clara's unusual abilities is to "love her unconditionally and accept her as she was." Blanca and Alba learn that the impaired children to whom they teach ceramics "worked much better when they felt loved, and that the only way to communicate with them was through affection." This is a lesson that Esteban finally learns, when at last he manages to love his granddaughter Alba without the anger that has crippled the rest of his relationships.

Sex Roles

The struggle of women to achieve equality and self-determination forms an important part of the novel, and is reflected in the clashes of the various female characters against Esteban Trueba. Although Esteban believes that a woman's duty is "motherhood and the home," he recognizes that this role is a difficult one: "I would not have liked to be a woman," he says to Férula when she expresses her bitterness at having to stay with their infirm mother. Interestingly enough, Esteban has nothing but respect for the most unconventional woman he knows, Tránsito Soto, whose ambition has made her into a successful businesswoman. Nevertheless, he treats women like property, raping peasant women without guilt, paying female workers less than men, and expecting his female relatives to obey his orders without question. He frowns on Nívea del Valle, who fights for the right to vote, and forbids Clara to teach the hacienda's workers about women's rights. Clara continually defies her husband's expectations, however, and essentially lives her life as she wants to, using his house to hold spiritualist sessions and minister to the poor. Blanca similarly defies her father by taking Pedro Tercero for her lover, even though she gives in to Esteban by marrying Jean de Satigny. By the time his granddaughter grows up, Esteban "had finally come to accept … that not all women were complete idiots," and agrees that Alba "could enter one of the professions and make her living like a man." The struggle for equality has made women strong, however, as Alba discovers after she is rescued from the empty lot where the political police have dumped her. The woman who takes her in is "one of the stoical, practical women of our country," and the risks she takes to help a stranger make Alba realize that "the days of Colonel García and all those like him are numbered, because they have not been able to destroy the spirit of these women."

Topics for Further Study

- Read Gabriel García Márquez's novel *One Hundred Years of Solitude*, to which *The House of the Spirits* has often been compared, if not accused of imitating. Make a note of the comparisons and the differences between the two works. In an essay, argue whether or not Allende's work is more than just an imitation of García Márquez's novel. Support your argument with examples.

- Research the history of Chile during the administration of Salvador Allende. Create a month-by-month timeline that illustrates the major developments—such as strikes or congressional actions—that led to the fall of his government. In a different color, add events from the novel that correspond to these developments.

- Do some research on the Internet and find a sampling of domestic violence statistics from various countries and cultures around the world. For those countries you select, also find out what kinds of laws protect the legal rights of women. Draw up a chart with your findings. Is there a correlation between women's legal status and domestic violence? Report your conclusion in a short essay.

- Author Gabriel García Márquez has said the key to writing in the magic realist style is to report on fantastic events with a perfectly "straight face." Start with an everyday subject, like a day at school or a meeting with friends, and try writing your own short story in the style of "magical realism."

- In *The House of the Spirits*, the character Clara demonstrates mental powers such as the ability to predict the future (clairvoyance), move objects (telekinesis), and communicate without words (telepathy). Investigate the history of such extrasensory perception (ESP). In an essay, compare previous scientific inquiries into ESP with what researchers believe today.

Justice and Injustice

Just as Esteban believes that women have their place in life, he also feels strongly about the role of the "lower classes." He believes his tenants "are like children, they can't handle responsibility," and is leery of letting them learn more than basic reading and math skills "for fear they would fill their minds with ideas unsuited to their station and condition." He does not recognize the injustice that his *patrón* system perpetuates and is unable to see in the intelligent Pedro Segundo "any virtues beyond those that marked him as a good peon." The clear-seeing Clara, however, recognizes the injustices created by class differences. As a young girl she sees the "absurdity" in her upper-class mother preaching about oppression and inequality to "hardworking women in denim aprons, their hands red with chilblains." When she takes Blanca with her to visit the poor, she explains that "this is to assuage our conscience…. But it doesn't help the poor. They don't need charity; they need justice." The election of the Socialist Candidate does little to ease class inequities, however, as the upper-class Conservatives conspire to undermine the government by arranging food shortages. After the coup, food returns to stores but the poor cannot afford it, and Alba sees a return to "the old days when her Grandmother Clara went to the Misericordia District to replace justice with charity." But, as the upper class discovers, the coup does not mean a return to the old class order; instead, the military forms a new class: they were "a breed apart, brothers who spoke a different dialect from civilians." Esteban García is a member of this new ruling class, and it is his perverted desire for "justice"—fed by his grandmother Pancha's tales of his parentage—that leads him to torture Alba. She comes to understand that the Colonel's purpose was not to gain information about Miguel, "but to avenge himself for injuries that had been inflicted on him from birth."

Science and Technology

The twentieth century is one of "light, science, and technology," as Severo del Valle believes. Esteban Trueba is similarly enchanted with scientific developments, and attempts to improve life at Tres Marías through technology. Science is not perfect, however, as it can do nothing to cure Clara's silence or discover why Esteban is shrinking. Similarly, many scientific improvements to the hacienda end up useless, such as the kerosene stove that becomes a henhouse because no one can learn how to use it. Old Pedro García often demonstrates the limits of science, as he dispels the hacienda's ant plague just by talking to the insects and sets Esteban's broken bones by touch so well that "the doctors who examined Trueba afterward could not believe such a thing was possible." Science and magic are not so different from each other, however. If sufficiently advanced, science becomes a kind of magic, as one cannot understand how it works and must take it on faith. Thus Father Restrepo calls the del Valle car "satanic," while the peasants of Tres Marías believe the news reports on the radio are "fairy tales, which did nothing to alter the narrowness of their existence." Clara recognizes this connection between science and magic: "If you can't understand how the telephone works," she tells Nicolás during his fruitless attempts to develop psychic powers, "how do you expect to understand miracles?"

Language and Meaning

Words and stories have a special significance in *The House of the Spirits*. Old Pedro García is respected and loved for his storytelling ability, and Nívea tells young Clara wild stories about their family in the hope that she will ask questions and thus regain her speech. Férula is such a gifted storyteller that "her listener felt as if he were there," and Pedro Tercero's story-songs create more converts than all the pamphlets he distributes. Language has power, and Clara believes that "by giving problems a name they tended to manifest themselves …; whereas if they remained in the limbo of unspoken words, they could disappear by themselves." Names have importance as well, as the names of Clara, Blanca, and Alba form "a chain of luminous words" which connect them to each other. Clara is convinced that Spanish and Esperanto are the only languages of interest to beings from other dimensions, while Esteban believes that English is superior to Spanish in describing the world of science and technology.

It is the written word, however, that has the most significance in the novel—after all, the family's story could not have been retold without Clara's notebooks, which "bore witness to life." Uncle Marcos's books of travel and fairy tales "inhabit the dreams of his descendants," giving Clara, Blanca, and Alba a shared mythology. The writing in Clara's notebooks reflects her state of mind, and her correspondence with Blanca "salvaged events from the mist of improbable facts." Jaime constructs a room with books, and Nicolás fills fifteen hundred pages with a treatise on spirituality. Even the government recognizes the might of the written word: "With the stroke of a pen the military changed world history, erasing every incident, ideology, and historical figure of which they disapproved." When the political police come for Alba, the culmination of their destruction comes when they set "an infamous pyre" that was fed with Jaime's collection, Uncle Marcos's books, Nicolás's treatise, and "even Trueba's opera scores." Thus, it is fitting that Alba battles this violence through writing, as both Clara's ghost and Ana Díaz suggest to her. Using Clara's notebooks, Blanca's letters, and other family documents, Alba can come to understand and survive through writing: "I write, she wrote, that memory is fragile and the space of a single life is brief, passing so quickly that we never get a chance to see the relationship between events…. I want to think that my task is life and that my mission is not to prolong hatred but simply to fill these pages."

Narration/Point of View

While much of *The House of the Spirits* seems to have very straightforward third-person ("he/she") narration, in fact there are three distinct narrative voices in the novel. The first voice is that of an unnamed first person ("I") narrator whom the reader does not discover is Alba until the epilogue. From this narrator's opening paragraph, the reader is made aware that this account has been reconstructed from Clara's notebooks. After this disclosure, however, the majority of reconstruction is told in the third person, with all characters referred to as "he" or "she." This second narrative voice is omniscient, or "all-knowing," able to relate what the various characters are thinking or feeling. This method of telling a story as a re-creation is not so unusual, except that it is interrupted at times by yet another narrative voice. This third voice belongs to Esteban Trueba, whose first person ("I") accounts serve to express either his intense passion or his acute suffering. (It is also interesting that all but the first of Esteban's encounters with Tránsito Soto are told in his voice.) Esteban's first-person accounts serve two purposes: first, they reinforce the idea that the novel has been reconstructed from the family histories, both written and oral. More important, however, is the way in which Esteban's words reveal the emotions he does not express in front of others. Without Esteban's narration, it would be easy to dismiss him as a cruel, heartless tyrant; including his heartfelt declarations, however, shows him to be a complex character struggling to battle his inner demons of passion and anger.

Setting

Although the setting of the novel is never explicitly named as Chile, the history of that country forms an important part of the plot. The political turmoil that engulfed Chile in the 1970s after the election of "the Candidate" Salvador Allende is reflected in the increasing impact that political events have in the lives of the characters. The more specific settings of the novel, however, have their own significance as well. The Tres Marías hacienda provides a good setting for illustrating the class conflict that is an important theme in the novel. Pedro Tercero's ability to come and go as he pleases from the hacienda reflects his more direct challenges to Esteban Trueba's authority. Similarly, "the battle of the sexes is cleverly manifested in the continuous struggle for space in the house," as Ronie-Richelle García-Johnson notes in *Revista Hispanica Moderna*. Esteban has designed the "big house on the corner" to demonstrate his own wealth and power, but it more accurately reflects the personality of his wife, Clara. Even when he is turning the salon of the house into a political meeting place, Clara manages to continue her spiritualist meetings and charity work by adding rooms and staircases to the back of the house. The split between the couple caused by Esteban's violence also becomes evident in the house, as "an invisible border arose between the parts of the house occupied by Esteban Trueba and those occupied by his wife." Little Alba recognizes that "her grandmother was the soul of the big house on the corner," and the loss Esteban feels after her death is mirrored in a similar decline of the house.

Foreshadowing

Foreshadowing is the technique of hinting at future events or setting up an explanation of later developments. Allende frequently uses foreshadowing in *The House of the Spirits* to hint at the fate facing her characters. The foreshadowing occurs not only in Clara's prophecies, but also in direct comments by the narrator. As early as Chapter 1, the narrator remarks that Rosa's poisoning is just "the first of many acts of violence that marked the fate of the del Valle family." A more specific remark comes in Chapter 7, when after reuniting with her brother Miguel after his first day of school, Amanda impulsively tells him that she would sacrifice herself for him. When the narrator adds that "she did not know then that one day she would have to," this anticipates Amanda's end, when she dies in police custody during questioning about her brother. Another instance of foreshadowing occurs at the end of Chapter 12, when the last surviving Mora sister comes to warn Alba that she is in danger. Esteban dismisses her words as crazy, but, the narrator notes, "later he would recall Luisa Mora's prophetic words, when they took Alba away in the middle of the night, while the curfew was in force." The frequent use of foreshadowing throughout the novel helps create a sense of fate at work and reinforces the violence of the political system, as the reader is constantly reminded that despite magical or pleasant interludes, dire events are yet to come.

Magical Realism

Because of its mixture of realistic everyday events with supernatural occurrences, *The House of the Spirits* fits within the literary genre known as magic realism or magical realism. A term first coined by Cuban writer Alejo Carpentier, magical realism is a style of writing which treats myth and magic with the same acceptance and objectivity as "truth." The abilities that allow Clara to play the piano with the cover closed and predict the future are just a few of the magical elements that appear in the novel. The Mora sisters possess a photograph containing "irrefutable proof that souls can take on physical form," and Férula's ghost appears to the entire family to announce her death. Every time Esteban comes to the big house, Blanca's rubber plant "lowered its leaves and began to exude a whitish fluid, like tears of milk, from its stem." *The House of the Spirits*, however, is much more frankly realistic in its portrayal of political turmoil than many other works of magical realism. There are almost no magical incidents in the later portions of the novel, particularly after the coup that leads to political repression. While this wide difference in tone may seem out of place, it actually serves to heighten the horror of the military's regime. Which is really more unbelievable, the author seems to be asking, a woman with psychic abilities or a government that tortures and murders thousands of its citizens?

Chile and the Turmoil of the 1970s

Although the setting of *The House of the Spirits* is never explicitly named, there are several historical events—from the 1933 earthquake to the election and overthrow of Salvador Allende—that clearly place the action in Chile. Occupying most of the southeastern coast of South America, Chile was part of the territory conquered by the Spanish in the 1500s. The country formally declared independence in 1818, but the nineteenth century was marked by both internal and external conflicts. By the 1910s, when the novel opens, Chile had enjoyed several years of relative peace and prosperity. The country's deposits of nitrate—an essential component of gunpowder—proved profitable during World War I. The wealth did not spread to workers such as miners, farm laborers, and factory workers, and so in the 1920s the country entered a period of strikes and political conflict which saw an increase in the kinds of radical political movements which so disturb Esteban Trueba throughout the novel. Salvador Allende was the cofounder of one of these parties, the Socialist Party, and was elected to the Chilean national congress in 1937 and to the senate in 1945. It was as a Socialist that he ran for president in four consecutive elections: 1952, 1958, 1964, and 1970. At the front of a Leftist coalition, Allende came in a close second in the 1958 election, but it was the 1970 election that finally brought him to power.

In a three-way race, Allende's Unidad Popular alliance won 36.3% of the popular vote—more than any other candidate, but not the majority required for election. Congress awarded him the presidency, but only after Allende signed a series of constitutional amendments that promised to protect the basic freedoms of political parties, labor unions, the media, and civic organizations. Allende's attempts to effect a peaceful transition to socialism —including the redistribution of land to peasants and the nationalization of businesses—were undercut by a broad array of forces, however. Radicals in his party led thousands of illegal land seizures and openly thwarted the president's efforts to compromise with the opposition in Congress. Wealthy Conservatives undermined the government by decreasing food production and encouraging trucking strikes that created food shortages. Several American business interests, worried about losing holdings to nationalization, encouraged the delay or cancellation of loans to Chile and even actively tried to subvert the government. The American Central Intelligence Agency, concerned about the spread of Communism, tried to bribe Chilean Congress members to prevent Allende from becoming president and unsuccessfully encouraged the Chilean military to overthrow the regime. By 1973, Allende's support had eroded: strikes were widespread, terrorism was waged by both right and left, and in June a tank regiment attacked the presidential palace. Hoping to restore order, Allende named the commanders of the armed forces to his cabinet that August. After congressional opposition called on the military to restore civil order, Allende's military ministers resigned and conservative forces in the military gave the president an ultimatum to resign. When Allende refused, the military took control of the government on September 11. Allende died during an attack on the presidential palace, the victim of either a self-inflicted gunshot wound (as the military claimed) or a military execution (as his allies and family alleged).

The military established a new government, led by General Augusto Pinochet, and moved quickly to stifle dissent. An estimated five to fifteen thousand Chileans were killed or tortured, or "disappeared," during and immediately after the coup; thousands of others fled into exile. Political parties, the Congress, trade unions, and any other organizations that opposed Pinochet were soon outlawed, and as many as forty thousand Chileans were arrested. Under the military government, torture became an accepted practice during the interrogation of political prisoners. In 1980, Pinochet imposed a new constitution that included a weak Congress with many members chosen undemocratically by the regime. The constitution also allowed military vetoes of most congressional decisions and allowed the government to suspend civil rights to deal with threats to "national security." While the regime's strict control initially led to improvements in Chile's economy, the upturn only benefited a small portion of the population. By 1982, the year *The House of the Spirits* was published, an international recession made it clear that the economic benefits of Pinochet's dictatorship were paltry, especially when compared to the loss of freedoms suffered by Chileans. Massive protests occurred, and in 1983 the military cracked down once again. Pinochet's 1980 constitution had allowed for a plebiscite in 1988, however, when the public would say "yes" or "no" to another term in office for the general. Pinochet was firmly convinced he would win, and allowed the vote to take place. A majority voted "no," and Pinochet agreed to step down. In presidential elections the following year, Pinochet's candidate lost to Patricio Aylwin. The return to democracy was peaceful, although Pinochet retained his position as leader of the military and opposed efforts to prosecute it for human rights abuses. World attention was focused on the brutality of Pinochet's regime in 1998, however, when he faced extradition from England to Spain to answer charges of assassination and torture.

Compare & Contrast

- **Chile:** The country of Chile occupies 748,800 square kilometers of land—roughly twice the size of Montana—and in the late 1990s had an estimated population of just over 14.5 million people.
  United States: The United States covers 9,158,960 square kilometers

of land, and in the late 1990s had an estimated population of over 270 million people.

- **Chile:** With a long history of political activism, modern-day Chile has over half a dozen different political parties; in order to form majority governments, however, these parties come together in two coalitions: the Coalition of Parties for Democracy (CPD) and the Union for the Progress of Chile (UPP).
  United States: Politics in the United States are controlled by two political groups: the Republican Party and the Democratic Party. While there have been several third-party movements throughout the twentieth century, none has seriously influenced the outcome of national elections since Theodore Roosevelt's Bull Moose Party during the presidential election of 1912.

- **Chile:** While the Chilean economy has opened up more to world trade since President Augusto Pinochet left office, the country's economy is still strongly dependent on natural resources—particularly copper mining, fishing, and forestry. In 1996, the estimated gross domestic product per person was $8,400.

United States: America enjoys one of the most powerful, diverse, and technologically advanced economies in the world. In 1997, the estimated gross domestic product per person was $30,200.

- **Chile:** At the end of 1998, the most controversial issue facing Chile was the proposed extradition of former President Augusto Pinochet from England to face charges of human rights abuses. Supporters of the General considered the action a blow to Chile's sovereignty, while his opponents argued that dictators should be held legally responsible for atrocities committed during their regimes.

  United States: At the end of 1998, the most controversial issue facing the American government was the impeachment of President Bill Clinton over his attempts to conceal an inappropriate relationship with a White House intern. Supporters of the president said the charges were trumped up by political opponents, while his opponents maintained that Clinton had obstructed justice and abused his power in trying to keep his actions secret.

"The Poet" and the Latin American "Boom"

Throughout *The House of the Spirits*, Allende frequently makes reference to "the Poet," a man revered and respected for his work. Even the Count de Satigny, a European, says the Poet's work "was the best poetry ever written, and that even in French, the language of the arts, there was nothing to compare it to." By the time Jaime and Nicolás are adults, the Poet is "a world-renowned figure, as Clara had predicted the first time she heard him recite in his telluric voice at one of her literary soirées." While the Poet is never named in the novel, it is clear that Allende is referring to Pablo Neruda, a Chilean poet who won the Nobel Prize for Literature in 1971. Neruda was not Chile's first Nobel laureate—poet Gabriela Mistral won the accolade in 1945—but he is considered one of the most important Latin American poets of the twentieth century. His works included such classics as *Residencia en la tierra* ("Residence on Earth," 1933), *Alturas de Macchu-Picchu* ("The Heights of Macchu Picchu," 1948), and his epic *Canto general de Chile* ("General Song of Chile," 1943, revised 1950). Through these works and many others, Neruda became noted worldwide for his innovative techniques and explorations of love, death, and the human condition. Neruda was a dedicated Communist who was nominated for president in 1970, but ended his candidacy and threw his support to the eventual winner, Salvador Allende. Neruda died less than two weeks after the military overthrow of Allende's government, and in the novel his funeral becomes "the symbolic burial of freedom."

Neruda was not the only Latin American writer to receive international recognition, however. The 1960s saw the beginning of the "Boom" in Latin American literature that brought numerous translations of Spanish-language works to English-speaking readers and critics. Writers such as Argentinean Jorge Luis Borges, Guatemalan Miguel Angel Asturias (Nobel, 1967), Colombian Gabriel García Máquez (Nobel, 1982), Peruvian Mario Vargas Llosa, and Mexicans Octavio Paz (Nobel, 1990) and Carlos Fuentes became familiar names to readers and academics. By the 1980s, most of the works by these well-known writers were appearing in translation and some were even adapted as English-language films. Few women writers emerged from the Boom, however, and so when the translation of Allende's *House of the Spirits* was published 1985, it was justly hailed for bringing a fresh, feminine perspective to the portrayal of Latin American life.

Critical Overview

Because of the author's family background and the political subject matter of *The House of the Spirits*, Allende's best-selling first novel was bound to cause a stir in literary circles. Most initial reviews of the work made it clear, however, that it was the author's talent, not her political credentials, that made *The House of the Spirits* well worth the wide readership it attained. *Washington Post Book World* critic Jonathan Yardley explained that "*The House of the Spirits* does contain a certain amount of rather predictable politics, but the only cause it wholly embraces is that of humanity, and it does so with such passion, humor and wisdom that in the end it transcends politics; it is also a genuine rarity, a work of fiction that is both an impressive literary accomplishment and a mesmerizing story fully accessible to a general readership." While observing that some of the minor characters are one-dimensional, *New York Times* reviewer Christopher Lehmann-Haupt added that "Clara, Blanca, and Alba Trueba ... are complex and vivid women. And the story's dominant character, the tragically ill-tempered Senator Esteban Trueba, is so appalling and appealing that he easily transcends ideology." "Slowly, this fine, stirring, generous novel casts its powerful spell," Hermione Lee stated in the *Observer*. While the critic expressed some reservations about Esteban's narration and the sentimental treatment of love, she noted that the novel "is a much more redoubtable and complex narrative, and much more grimly truthful, than at first appears."

Not all early reviews were positive, however. Paul West attributed the "runaway vogue" of *The House of the Spirits* to the popularity of the family chronicle genre and found that the magical elements detracted from the focus on the characters. "As *The House of the Spirits* advances," the critic wrote in the *Nation*, "it calms down into the book Allende probably wanted to write, and would have had she not felt obliged to toe the line of magical realism." D. A. N. Jones similarly objected to the magical elements, writing in the *London Review of Books* that "bizarre little fantasies come sputtering out with an inconsequential brevity, like ideas thrown up at a script conference for a Latin American soap opera or horror film." But other critics praised what *Chicago Tribune Book World* contributor Bruce Allen called "Allende's gift for dramatic detail": "The most remarkable feature of this remarkable book," the critic explained, "is the way in which its strong political sentiments are made to coexist with its extravagant and fascinating narrative." Suzanne Ruta similarly observed that Allende's "fidelity to the magic realist formula ... worked because history provided ample ballast and counterweight to her flights of fancy." While there is "something a bit precious about the story of grandmother Clara, mother Blanca, and daughter Alba," the critic concluded in the *Women's Review of Books* that "it took courage to turn the ugly reality of 1973 and after into a kind of fairy tale. I read it and wept."

Because of its style and plot, it was inevitable that many reviewers would make comparisons between Allende's novel and Colombian author Gabriel García Máquez's masterpiece *One Hundred Years of Solitude*. *Village Voice* contributor Enrique Fernández, for instance, stated that "only the dullest reader can fail to be distracted by the shameless cloning from *One Hundred Years of Solitude*." While faulting the ending of the novel for using one of García Máquez's "hoariest clichés"—the discovery of a manuscript—*Time* critic Patricia Blake noted that "Allende is not just an epigone [poor imitator] of García Máquez. Writing in the tradition of Latin America's magic realists, she has a singular talent for producing full-scale representational portraits with comic surreal touches." Many other critics agreed that while Allende may have used *One Hundred Years* as a model, *The House of the Spirits* is her own unique achievement. A *Publishers Weekly* reviewer made the comparison with García Máquez and declared that "Allende has her own distinctive voice, however; while her prose lacks the incandescent brilliance of the master's, it has a whimsical charm, besides being clearer, more accessible, and more explicit about the contemporary situation in South America." *New York Times Book Review* contributor Alexander Coleman likewise remarked that Allende's work differs from the fatalism of García Márquez's work in that it is "a novel of peace and reconciliation, in spite of the fact that it tells of bloody, tragic events. The author has accomplished this not only by plumbing her memory for the familial and political textures of the continent, but also by turning practically every major Latin American novel on its head." The critic added: "Rarely has a new novel from Latin America consciously or unconsciously owed more to its predecessors; equally rare is the original utterance coming out of what is now a collective literary inheritance." In a *Latin American Literary Review* article devoted to comparing the two works, Robert Antoni determined that there are significant differences, including the feminine, first-person voice; the presentation of Clara's manuscript as history, not prediction; and the interesting dialogue created by including Esteban Trueba's voice in the narrative. In Allende's work "historical writing replaces magical writing, tragic sentiments replace comic sentiments," the critic concluded. "All this amounts to a novel which—more consciously than unconsciously—may begin as an attempt to rewrite *One Hundred Years of Solitude*, but which discovers itself as a unique statement."

Further assessments of the novel have examined it from a feminist perspective, analyzing the author's depiction of the patriarchal society of Latin America. Critics have also paid attention to the role that writing and storytelling play in the novel, thus presenting an examination of the nature and uses of art. Reviewers have generally come to value *The House of the Spirits* not only as a commentary on turbulent political times in Chile but also as a powerful piece of humanistic fiction. Sara Maitland noted in the *New Statesman* that *The House of the Spirits* "seemed to me to take South

American 'magic realism' a step further in the direction I have always felt it could go—to a fictional technique which can carry universal meaning within its own specific location of character and place." Coleman suggested that *The House of the Spirits* is well worth comparison with the best works of the Latin American "Boom." As he concluded in the *New York Times Book Review*, Allende is "the first woman to approach on the same scale as the others the tormented patriarchal world of traditional Hispanic society and to argue that the enraged class violence in Latin America is a debate among men who are not only deaf but who have fixed and unalterable ideas on all subjects. And she has done all this in an absorbing and distinguished work that matches her predecessors' in quality as well as scope."

Sources

Bruce Allen, "A Magical Vision of Society in Revolt," *Chicago Tribune Book World*, May 19, 1985, pp. 37-38.

Isabel Allende, "Sobre *La casa de los espíritus*" (Spanish language), *Discurso Literario*, Vol. 2, Autumn, 1984, pp. 67-73.

Robert Antoni, "Parody or Piracy: The Relationship of *The House of the Spirits* to *One Hundred Years of Solitude*," *Latin American Literary Review*, Vol. XVI, No. 32, July-December, 1988, pp. 16-28.

Patricia Blake, "From Chile with Magic," *Time*, Vol. 125, No. 20, May 20, 1985, p. 79.

Alexander Coleman, "Reconciliation among the Ruins," *New York Times Book Review*, May 12, 1985, pp. 1, 22-23.

Enrique Fernández, "Send in the Clone," *Village Voice*, Vol. XXX, No. 23, June 4, 1985, p. 51.

Ronie-Richelle García-Johnson, "The Struggle for Space: Feminism and Freedom," *Revista Hispanica Moderna*, Columbia University Hispanic Studies, Vol. XLVII, No. 1, June, 1994, pp 184-93.

Review of *The House of the Spirits, Publishers Weekly*, Vol. 227, No. 9, March 1, 1985, p. 70.

D. A. N. Jones, "Magical Realism," *London Review of Books*, August 1, 1985, pp. 26-7.

Hermione Lee, "Chile Con Carnage," *Observer*, June 7, 1985, p. 21.

Christopher Lehmann-Haupt, Review of *The House of the Spirits, New York Times*, May 9, 1985, p. 23.

Sara Maitland, "Courage and Convictions," *New Statesman*, Vol. 114, No. 2937, July 10, 1987, p. 27.

Suzanne Ruta, "Lovers and Storytellers," *Women's Review of Books*, Vol. VIII, No. 9, June, 1991, p. 10.

Amanda Smith, "PW Interviews: Isabel Allende," *Publishers Weekly*, May 7, 1985.

Paul West, "Narrative Overdrive," *Nation*, Vol. 241, No. 2, July 20 & 27, 1985, pp. 52-4.

Jonathan Yardley, "Desire and Destiny in Latin America," *Washington Post Book World*, May 12, 1985, pp. 3-4.

For Further Study

Robert M. Adams, "The Story Isn't Over," in *New York Review of Books*, Vol. XXXII, No. 12, July 18, 1985, pp. 20-23.

> Mixed review of the novel that praises Allende's use of magical elements and mood of reconciliation. The critic does fault the author for failing to take proper advantage of her eccentric but "entertaining" female characters.

Lori M. Carlson, review of *The House of the Spirits*, in *Review*, No. 34, January-June, 1985, pp. 77-78.

> Praises Allende's "precise structuring of character development" and notes that the novel remains compelling even if very reminiscent of García Márquez's *One Hundred Years of Solitude*.

Susan de Carvalho, "Escrituras y Escritoras: The Artist-Protagonist of Isabel Allende," in *Discurso Literario*, Vol. 10, No. 1, 1992, pp. 59-67.

> Examines the self-exploration of the narrators in Allende's *Eva Luna* and *The House of the Spirits*.

P. Gabrielle Foreman, "Past-On Stories: History and the Magically Real, Morrison and Allende on Call," in *Feminist Studies*, Vol. 18, No. 2, Summer, 1992, pp 369-88.

Comparative study in which Foreman examines the "interrelation of history, ontology, and the magically real" in Allende's *The House of the Spirits* and Toni Morrison's *Beloved*.

Ambrose Gordon, "Isabel Allende on Love and Shadow," in *Contemporary Literature*, Vol. 28, No. 4, Winter, 1987, pp 530-42.

A review of Allende's second novel, *Of Love and Shadows*, that includes a generally positive assessment of *The House of the Spirits*. Gordon notes that the novel's "bizarre detail" and "jumbled history" do not necessarily mean the work is not valuable. Concludes that the novel works as a skillful "weapon" of protest against the Pinochet government.

Patricia Hart, *Narrative Magic in the Fiction of Isabel Allende*, Fairleigh Dickinson University Press, 1989.

A book-length study of the magic realist elements of Allende's work.

Ruth Y. Jenkins, "Authorizing Female Voice and Experience: Ghosts and Spirits in Kingston's *The Woman Warrior* and Allende's *The House of the Spirits*," in *Melus*, Vol. 19, No. 3, Fall, 1994, pp.

61-73.

> Examines the "connections between the supernatural and female voice" in Allende's *The House of the Spirits* and Maxine Hong Kingston's *The Woman Warrior*, stating that "both authors narrate and preserve authentic female experience."

Claudia Marie Kovach, "Mask and Mirror: Isabel Allende's Mechanism for Justice in *The House of the Spirits*," in *Post-colonial Literature and the Biblical Call for Justice*, University Press of Mississippi, 1994, pp. 74-90.

> Examines the ways in which Allende propagates a "prophetic vision of female integrity and justice" in *The House of the Spirits*, focusing on the role of memories in the book and Allende's narrative strategies.

Marilyn Berlin Snell, "The Shaman and the Infidel," in *New Perspectives Quarterly*, Vol. 8, No. 1, Winter, 1991, pp. 54-58.

> Interview in which Allende discusses Latin American literature, magic realism, and the major themes of her work.

Gail Tayko, "Teaching Isabel Allende's *La casa de los espíritus*," in *College Literature*, Vols. 19-20, Nos. 3-1, October, 1992–February, 1993, pp 228-32.

Discusses how *The House of the Spirits* could be utilized in the classroom, concluding that the work "interweaves sexual, political, and economic oppression and affirms the national identity of Chile through its focus on the familial sphere. In doing so the novel powerfully raises the issues that are so important for students to confront."

Michael Toms, interview with Isabel Allende in *Common Boundary*, May/June, 1994, pp. 16-23.

An interview in which Allende discusses her writing technique, how personal experience has affected her works, her literary influences, and her career as a journalist Robert Wilson, "A Latin Epic of Marxism and Magic," in *USA Today*, June 7, 1985, p. 4D.

Mostly positive review of the novel that nevertheless faults the author's treatment of President Allende's rise and fall for leaving her characters behind.